Rain Forest Discovery

Jo Weaver
Illustrated by Pat Reynolds

Contents

Chapter 1

Fall Vacation

Jess and her parents were on a weekend vacation in late September. They were staying near the Nature Center in a rain forest in Washington State.

One morning Jess and her mom and dad got up early. They were going on a hike in the forest with one of the forest rangers.

At the Nature Center, they met Ranger Kelly. She talked about some of the animals they might see on their hike. She told them they would need to look closely and listen carefully.

"Okay, let's get going," said Ranger Kelly. "Follow me!"

"I hope we see a deer!" said Jess.

"Maybe we'll see an owl," said Dad.

"I'd like to see a flying squirrel," said Mom.

6

"Owls hunt flying squirrels
for food," said Ranger Kelly.

"But owls and flying squirrels
only come out at night," said Jess.

"Really?" said Mom.

"That's right," answered Ranger Kelly. "They are two of the many nocturnal animals in the rain forest."

"I don't think I'd like to walk through the rain forest at night!" said Dad.

Chapter 2

Into the Forest

Jess and her family followed Ranger Kelly along the trail. Sunlight came through the trees. It made beautiful patterns on the ground.

Jess looked up. She saw the tallest tree she had ever seen.

"Wow! What kind of tree is that?" she asked.

"It's a Sitka spruce," said Ranger Kelly. "It's almost 300 feet tall. That's as tall as a 30-story building!"

Jess looked through her binoculars.
She could see the top of the huge tree.
It reached higher than all the other trees.

"I don't see any birds or other animals
up there," she said.

"Many creatures blend in with the branches and leaves. That helps keep them safe," said Ranger Kelly. "So they might be there even though you can't see them. Keep looking!"

Jess and her mom and dad continued to walk farther into the forest with Ranger Kelly.

Jess stopped to close her eyes and listen. She could hear the sounds of many different birds and insects.

Suddenly, she heard a thump and then a rustling sound on the forest floor. She opened her eyes.

"What was that?" she asked.

"I don't know," replied Mom.
"Can you see anything?"

Chapter 3

The Discovery

Jess scanned the forest floor. Then she saw something almost buried in the leaves.

"Kelly," Jess called. "What's that over there in the leaves?"

Ranger Kelly looked where Jess
was pointing.

"Let's go and see, Jess," she said.
"But step carefully. Lots of plants
and animals live on the forest floor.
We don't want to hurt any of them."

Jess followed carefully in
Kelly's footsteps.

A small creature was almost
completely buried in the fallen
leaves and branches.

"What is it?" Jess whispered.

Her heart beat fast as Ranger Kelly stepped closer and moved the leaves away. Jess could see that the creature's heart was beating fast, too.
It was alive!

Chapter 4

The Rescue

"It's a young Spotted Owl, Jess," whispered Ranger Kelly. "It's only about five months old."

"The Spotted Owl is an endangered animal, isn't it?" whispered Jess.

Ranger Kelly nodded. "It sure is, Jess. And this young owl is injured. I think its wing might be broken."

"What should we do?" asked Jess.

"I'll call the Wildlife Care Center. One of their Animal Rescue teams will come and pick the owl up," said Ranger Kelly.

"It must be very scared," said Jess.

"Yes, that's why it's not moving much," Ranger Kelly whispered. "We can help by keeping it warm and in a dark place until help arrives."

Chapter 5

The Future

Ranger Kelly and Jess carefully made their way back to the trail.

"We found an injured Spotted Owl," Jess told her parents. "We called Animal Rescue, and they're on their way to help."

"Is it going to be okay?" asked Mom.

"I think so," replied Ranger Kelly. "The Wildlife Care Center will take care of it until its wing heals. Then it can be released back into its natural habitat."

They all waited for the Animal Rescue team to arrive. Ranger Kelly and Jess showed them where the owl had fallen.

"It's a good thing you heard it fall," said the man from Animal Rescue. "Many young owls don't survive in the wild—especially the ones that get injured."

"I'm just glad we could help it," said Jess.

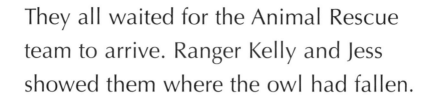

"You can visit the owl at the Center after it has healed a bit," said the woman from Animal Rescue.

"Really? That would be great," said Jess. "Thank you!"

"Would you like to finish our hike now?"
asked Ranger Kelly.

"I sure would!" said Jess. "There's so
much more to see and learn.
The rain forest is filled with wildlife!"

A Rain Forest Habitat

Rain forests are found in places where there is a lot of rain. Huge trees and many other plants grow in these forests. They provide shelter and food for the creatures that live in the rain forest habitat.

Temperate Rain Forest, Washington State, U.S.A.

The Spotted Owl

Spotted Owls live in rain forests in North America. They nest in old trees, where they sleep during the day. At night, they hunt for food.

Spotted Owls could become extinct if their habitat is not protected.

Northern Spotted Owl

Think About the Story

In *Rain Forest Discovery*, Jess and her mom and dad visit a rain forest. Think about these questions.

- What creatures do Jess and her mom and dad hope to see on their hike?
- Why do Jess and Ranger Kelly leave the trail? What do they find?
- How do Jess and Ranger Kelly help the injured creature?

To learn more about animal habitats, read the books below.

SUGGESTED READING
Windows on Literacy
The Rain Forest
Life in the Ocean

32